HAL•LEONARD®

VIOLIN
PLAY-ALONG

AUDIO
ACCESS
INCLUDED

VOL. 21

ANDREW LLOYD WEBBER™

T0131121

To access audio visit:
www.halleonard.com/mylibrary

Enter Code
3422-8437-3293-5023

Andrew Lloyd Webber™ is a trademark owned by Andrew Lloyd Webber.

The musical works contained in this edition may not be publicly performed in a dramatic form or context except under license from The Really Useful Group Limited, 22 Tower Street, London WC2H 9TW.

ISBN 978-1-61780-775-6

HAL•LEONARD®
CORPORATION

7777 W. BLUEMOUND RD. P.O. BOX 13819 MILWAUKEE, WI 53213

Violin by Jerry Loughney

CONTENTS

All I Ask of You

from THE PHANTOM OF THE OPERA

Music by Andrew Lloyd Webber
Lyrics by Charles Hart
Additional Lyrics by Richard Stilgoe

world with no more night; and you, al-ways be-side me, to hold me and to hide me. Then

say you'll share with me one love, one life-time; let me lead you from your

sol-i-tude. ___ Say you need me with you; here be-side you;

an-y-where you go, let me go too. Chris-tine, ___ that's all I ask of

Say you'll share with me one love, one life-time; say the word and I will
you.

fol-low you. ___ Share each day with me, each night, each morn-ing. Say you love me!
You know I

do. Love me, that's all I ask of you.

An-y-where you go, let me go too; love me, that's all I ask of you.

Any Dream Will Do

from JOSEPH AND THE AMAZING TECHNICOLOR® DREAMCOAT
Music by Andrew Lloyd Webber
Lyrics by Tim Rice

Don't Cry for Me Argentina

from EVITA
Music by Andrew Lloyd Webber
Lyrics by Tim Rice

ti - na.   Mm. _____

Don't cry for me Ar - gen -

ti - na, _____   the truth is I nev - er   left you.   All through my   wild days, ___   my mad ex -

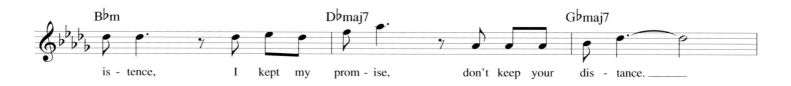

is - tence,   I kept my   prom - ise,   don't keep your   dis - tance. _____

Have   I   said   too much, there's noth - ing   more   I   can   think   of   to   say   to   you. __

But   all   you   have   to   do   is   look   at   me   to   know   that   ev - 'ry

word   is   true. __   _ff_

The Music of the Night

from THE PHANTOM OF THE OPERA
Music by Andrew Lloyd Webber
Lyrics by Charles Hart
Additional Lyrics by Richard Stilgoe

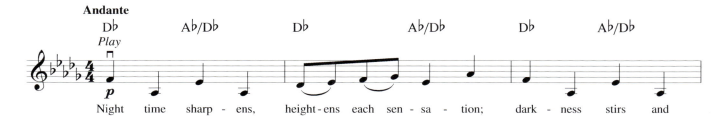

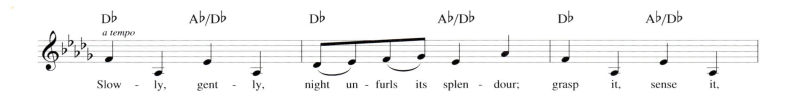

thoughts of the life you knew be - fore! Close your eyes let your spi - rit start to

soar and you'll live as you've nev - er lived be - fore.

Soft - ly, deft - ly, mu - sic shall ca - ress you. Hear it, feel it,

se - cret - ly pos - sess you. O - pen up your mind let your fan - ta - sies un - wind in this

dark - ness which you know you can - not fight, the dark - ness of the mu - sic of the

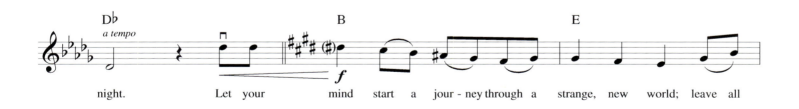

night. Let your mind start a jour - ney through a strange, new world; leave all

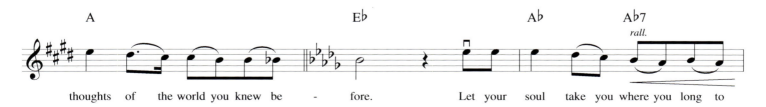

thoughts of the world you knew be - fore. Let your soul take you where you long to

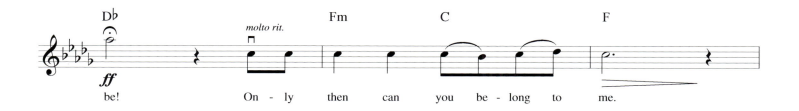

be! On - ly then can you be - long to me.

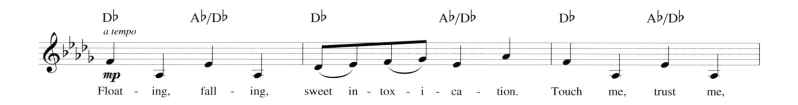

Float - ing, fall - ing, sweet in - tox - i - ca - tion. Touch me, trust me,

sa - vour each sen - sa - tion. Let the dream be - gin, let your dark - er side give in to the

pow - er of the mu - sic that I write, the pow - er of the mu - sic of the

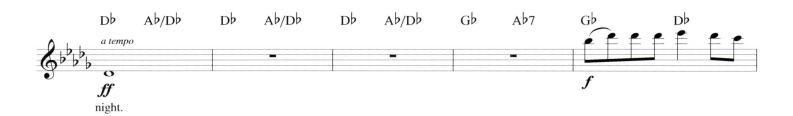

night.

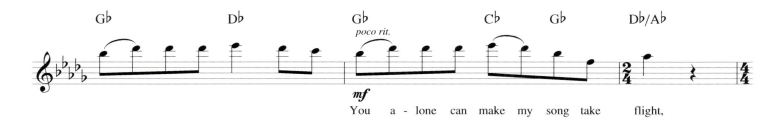

You a - lone can make my song take flight,

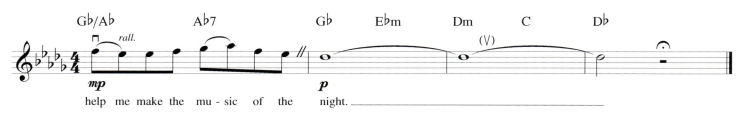

help me make the mu - sic of the night. _____

Memory

from CATS

Music by Andrew Lloyd Webber
Text by Trevor Nunn after T.S. Eliot

mem - o - ry too _____ and a new day _____ will be - gin.

Burnt out ends of smo - ky days, _____ the

stale cold smell _____ of morn - ing. _____ The street lamp dies, an - oth - er

night is o - ver, _____ an - oth - er day is dawn - ing.

Touch me. _____ It's so eas - y to leave me _____ all a - lone with the

mem - ory _____ of my days in the sun. _____ If you touch me you'll un - der-stand what

hap - pi - ness is. Look, a new day has be - gun.

The Phantom of the Opera

from THE PHANTOM OF THE OPERA
Music by Andrew Lloyd Webber
Lyrics by Charles Hart
Additional Lyrics by Richard Stilgoe and Mike Batt

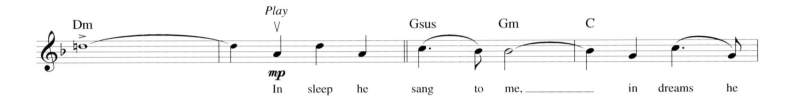

In sleep he sang to me, in dreams he

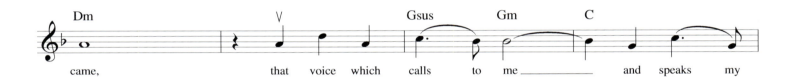

came, that voice which calls to me and speaks my

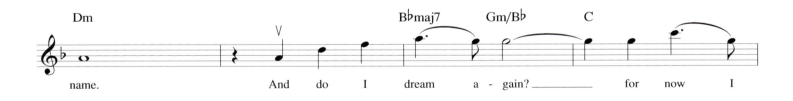

name. And do I dream a - gain? for now I

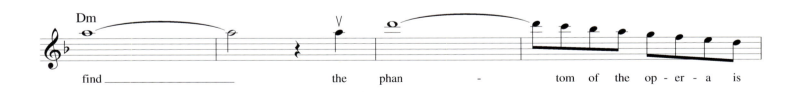

find the phan - tom of the op - er - a is

there in - side my mind.

Sing once a - gain with me

our strange du - et; my pow - er o - ver you grows strong - er

yet. And though you turn from me to glance be -

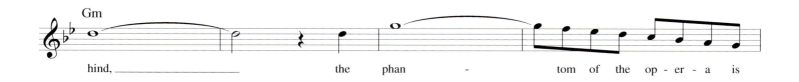

hind, the phan - tom of the op - er - a is

there in - side your mind.

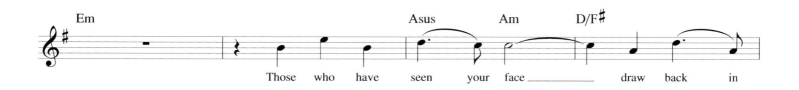

Those who have seen your face draw back in

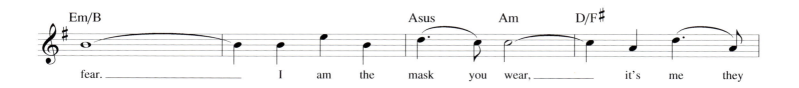

fear. I am the mask you wear, it's me they

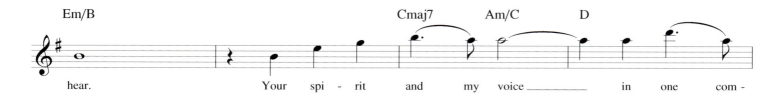

hear. Your spi - rit and my voice in one com -

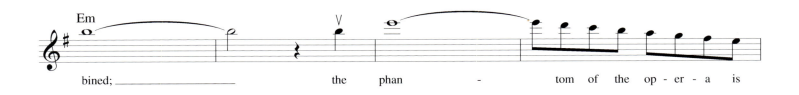

bined; _____ the phan - tom of the op - er - a is

there in - side my mind.

In all your

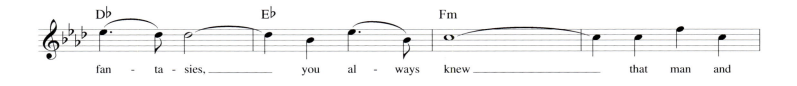

fan - ta - sies, _____ you al - ways knew _____ that man and

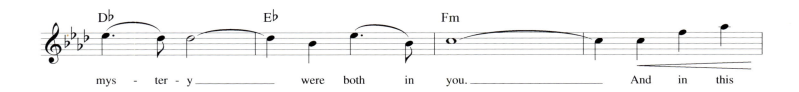

mys - ter - y _____ were both in you. _____ And in this

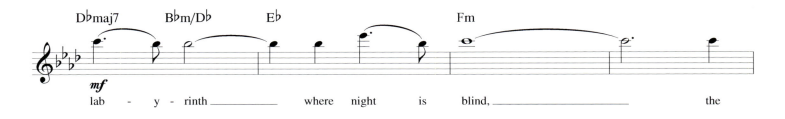

lab - y - rinth _____ where night is blind, _____ the

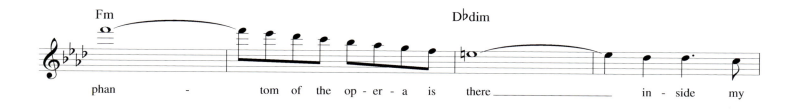

phan - tom of the op-er-a is there _____ in - side my

mind. He's

there, the phan - tom of the op - era. _____

Ah! _____

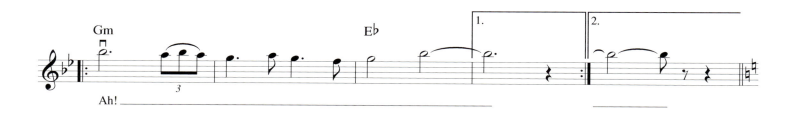

Ah! _____

Ah! _____

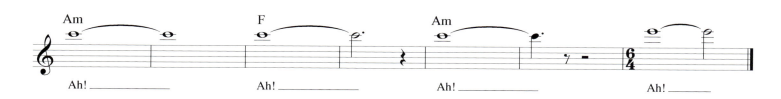

Ah! _____   Ah! _____   Ah! _____   Ah! _____

Unexpected Song

from SONG & DANCE
Music by Andrew Lloyd Webber
Lyrics by Don Black

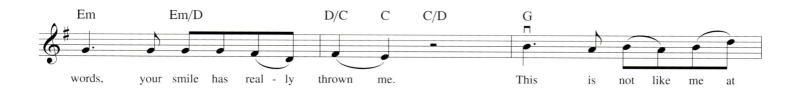

words,   your smile has real - ly   thrown me.   This   is   not like me at

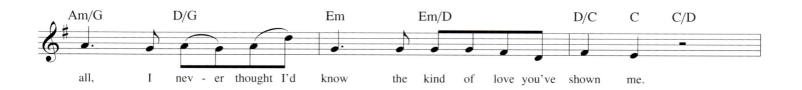

all,   I nev - er thought I'd   know   the kind of love you've shown me.

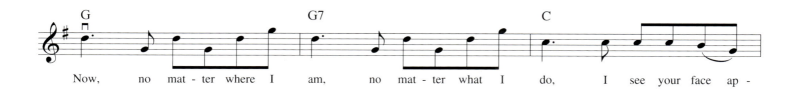

Now,   no mat - ter where I   am,   no mat - ter what I   do,   I   see your face ap -

pear - ing   like   an un - ex - pect - ed   song,   an un - ex - pect - ed

song   that on - ly we are hear - ing.   Like   an un - ex - pect - ed

song,   an un - ex - pect - ed   song   that on - ly we are hear - ing. _____

Whistle Down the Wind

from WHISTLE DOWN THE WIND
Music by Andrew Lloyd Webber
Lyrics by Jim Steinman

Moderato con moto

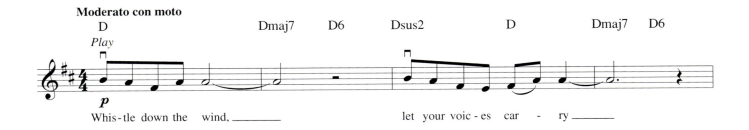

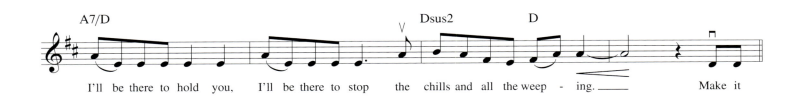

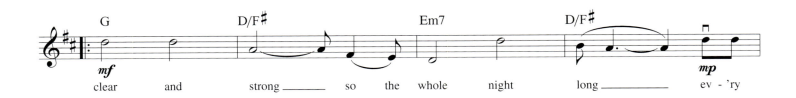

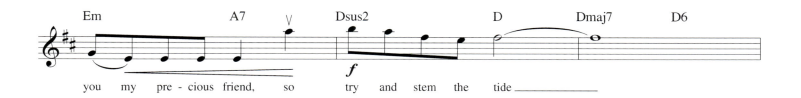

you my pre - cious friend, so try and stem the tide _____

then you'll raise a ban - ner _____ send a flare up in the sky, try to burn a torch and

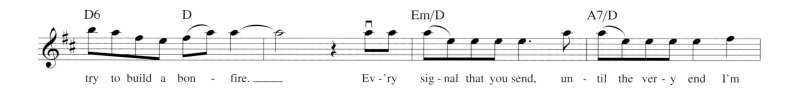

try to build a bon - fire. _____ Ev - 'ry sig - nal that you send, un - til the ver - y end I'm

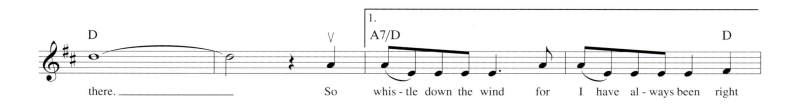

there. _____ So whis - tle down the wind for I have al - ways been right

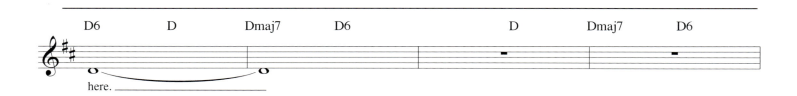

here. _____

Make it

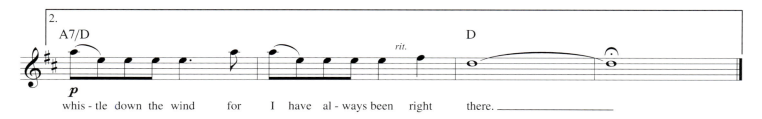

whis - tle down the wind for I have al - ways been right there. _____

HAL•LEONARD® VIOLIN PLAY-ALONG

AUDIO ACCESS INCLUDED

The Violin Play-Along Series

Play your favorite songs quickly and easily!

Just follow the music, listen to the CD or online audio to hear how the violin should sound, and then play along using the separate backing tracks. The audio files are enhanced so you can adjust the recordings to any tempo without changing pitch!

1. Bluegrass
00842152 ....$14.99

2. Popular Songs
00842153 ....$16.99

3. Classical
00842154 ....$16.99

4. Celtic
00842155 ....$14.99

5. Christmas Carols
00842156 ....$14.99

6. Classic Christmas Songs
00348311 ....$14.99

7. Jazz
00842196 ....$16.99

8. Country Classics
00842230 ....$14.99

9. Country Hits
00842231 ....$14.99

10. Bluegrass Favorites
00842232 ....$14.99

11. Bluegrass Classics
00842233 ....$16.99

12. Wedding Classics
00842324 ....$14.99

13. Wedding Favorites
00842325 ....$16.99

14. Blues Classics
00842427 ....$14.99

15. Stephane Grappelli
00842428 ....$16.99

16. Folk Songs
00842429 ....$14.99

17. Christmas Favorites
00842478 ....$14.99

18. Fiddle Hymns
00842499 ....$14.99

19. Lennon & McCartney
00842564 ....$14.99

20. Irish Tunes
00842565 ....$16.99

21. Andrew Lloyd Webber
00842566 ....$16.99

22. Broadway Hits
00842567 ....$14.99

23. Pirates of the Caribbean
00842625 ....$16.99

24. Rock Classics
00842640 ....$14.99

25. Classical Masterpieces
00842642 ....$14.99

26. Elementary Classics
00842643 ....$14.99

27. Classical Favorites
00842646 ....$14.99

28. Classical Treasures
00842647 ....$14.99

29. Disney Favorites
00842648 ....$16.99

30. Disney Hits
00842649 ....$14.99

31. Movie Themes
00842706 ....$14.99

32. Favorite Christmas Songs
00102110 ....$14.99

33. Hoedown
00102161 ....$14.99

34. Barn Dance
00102568 ....$14.99

35. Lindsey Stirling
00109715 ....$19.99

36. Hot Jazz
00110373 ....$14.99

37. Taylor Swift
00116361 ....$14.99

38. John Williams
00116367 ....$16.99

39. Italian Songs
00116368 ....$14.99

40. Trans-Siberian Orchestra
00119909 ....$19.99

41. Johann Strauss
00121041 ....$14.99

42. Light Classics
00121935 ....$14.99

43. Light Orchestra Pop
00122126 ....$14.99

44. French Songs
00122123 ....$14.99

45. Lindsey Stirling Hits
00123128 ....$19.99

46. Piazzolla Tangos
48022997 ....$16.99

47. Light Masterworks
00124149 ....$14.99

48. Frozen
00126478 ....$14.99

49. Pop/Rock
00130216 ....$14.99

50. Songs for Beginners
00131417 ....$14.99

51. Chart Hits for Beginners – 2nd Ed.
00293887 ....$14.99

52. Celtic Rock
00148756 ....$16.99

53. Rockin' Classics
00148768 ....$14.99

54. Scottish Folksongs
00148779 ....$14.99

55. Wicked
00148780 ....$14.99

56. The Sound of Music
00148782 ....$14.99

57. Movie Music
00150962 ....$14.99

58. The Piano Guys – Wonders
00151837 ....$19.99

59. Worship Favorites
00152534 ....$14.99

60. The Beatles
00155293 ....$16.99

61. Star Wars: The Force Awakens
00157648 ....$14.99

62. Star Wars
00157650 ....$14.99

63. George Gershwin
00159612 ....$14.99

64. Lindsey Stirling Favorites
00159634 ....$19.99

65. Taylor Davis
00190208 ....$19.99

66. Pop Covers
00194642 ....$14.99

67. Love Songs
00211896 ....$14.99

68. Queen
00221964 ....$14.99

69. La La Land
00232247 ....$17.99

70. Metallica
00242929 ....$14.99

71. Andrew Lloyd Webber Hits
00244688 ....$14.99

72. Lindsey Stirling – Selections from Warmer in the Winter
00254923 ....$19.99

73. Taylor Davis Favorites
00256297 ....$19.99

74. The Piano Guys – Christmas Together
00262873 ....$19.99

75. Ed Sheeran
00274194 ....$16.99

76. Cajun & Zydeco Songs
00338131 ....$14.99

77. Favorite Christmas Hymns
00278017 ....$14.99

78. Hillsong Worship Hits
00279512 ....$14.99

79. Lindsey Stirling – Top Songs
00284305 ....$19.99

80. Gypsy Jazz
00293922 ....$14.99

81. Lindsey Stirling – Christmas Collection
00298588 ....$19.99

www.halleonard.com